MADE FOR MORE

Living In The Purposes of God

Bishop Greg D. Gill

Copyright © 2025 by Greg D. Gill

Cover design by Bee Adufina, Happy Bee Productions

Book publishing services by Opulent Books www.OpulentBooks.net

All rights reserved.

ISBN Paperback: 978-1-916691-85-8

No part of this publication may be reproduced, distributed, or transmitted in any form or by any means, including photocopying, recording, or other electronic or mechanical methods, without the prior written permission of the publisher, except as permitted by copyright law. For permission requests, contact the author.

Scriptures are taken from the NEW INTERNATIONAL VERSION (NIV): Scripture taken from THE HOLY BIBLE, NEW INTERNATIONAL VERSION ®. Copyright© 1973, 1978, 1984, 2011 by Biblica, Inc.TM. Used by permission of Zondervan

Endorsements For *Made for More*

I've known Bishop Greg Gill for over 30 years, and what you read in this book reflects the passion and authenticity of his life. He doesn't just write about pursuing more of God—he lives it. This book will stir your heart, challenge your routines, and invite you into a deeper, more vibrant walk with Jesus. If you're hungry for more, this is a must-read.

Jason Persaud
Culture Changers
Brampton, Ontario, Canada

My friend, Bishop Greg, names what so many of us feel but rarely admit: the slow drift into spiritual autopilot. His words are both a timely wake-up call and a gracious invitation to rediscover the abundance of faith and the God who is always 'more.' I believe you will be truly blessed, inspired, and moved to make a fresh dedication in your walk with Christ as you read this.

Christine Martin
Pastor, Author, Speaker
Minneapolis, Minnesota, USA

In *Made for More*, Bishop Greg Gill has given the Body of Christ a timely word for this hour. With clarity, compassion, and conviction, he points us away from spiritual stagnation and toward ongoing transformation by the Spirit. This is not just a book—it is an invitation to pursue intimacy with God beyond measure. Every believer who longs for fresh fire and renewed passion should read this.

Ps Robin & Michelle Ramcharan
In The River
Cocoyea, San Fernando, Trinidad & Tobago

Do you need your faith to be stirred? Are you hungry to step into all that God has for you? God has made you for more, beyond all you can think or imagine. Bishop Greg has written a wonderful book that will stir your spirit, challenge you to surrender to Him, and help you walk in victory!

Rev. Randall Heier
Propel Church Global
Calgary, Alberta, Canada

Over 35 years ago, I met Bishop Greg Gill when we were students together, preparing for ministry. Even in those early days, he carried a deep passion for the things of God. There was a revival fire burning within him—a relentless hunger for MORE of God. Remarkably, that fire has never gone out.

Today, his passion for the fullness of God continues to burn brightly and impact lives around the world. In his new book, *Made for More*, we are invited to pursue that same fullness and to realize there truly is more available in God.

As you read, you will be inspired, challenged, and drawn into a deeper walk of faith. Bishop Gill pours out his heart in these pages, passionately calling every believer to rise to their maximum in Christ. Now is the time to chase after the MORE!

Rev. D. R. Young
Speaker, Counsellor, Author
Edmonton, Alberta, Canada

In *Made for More* Bishop Greg Gill lays down a clarion call, a veritable gauntlet, challenging readers to shake off complacency and press into a destiny of 'more.' With fear and trembling I read the word 'plateau,' nervous as a backslider at a prophetic conference—'not me, plateaued? Surely not!'

However, the real-life stories, combined with the usual apostolic precision, painted the canvas clearly with the symptoms I had ignored. It was a masterpiece of poignant words that resoundingly called for my attention to go deeper with God.

Thank the Lord for spiritual leaders who lovingly speak truth and call us out of complacency, call us higher, and inspire us to transform into MORE!

Rev. D. Mark Griffin
Itinerant Minister
Cobourg, Ontario, Canada

There comes a time in your life when you just know you were made for more. A deep groaning and desperation lies within you. It is not ordinary, not something you can easily shake off. That is the 'more of God' awakening inside of you—a faith that goes beyond limitations, barriers, and obstacles.

In this book *Made for More*, Bishop Greg Gill captures the urgency of our 'why.' He recalibrates, refocuses, and launches us into a greater awareness of our calling. This book is not simply informational, it is transformational. It provides the ingredients the Body of Christ needs to reclaim its God-given identity and authority.

Bishop Gill lays out solid principles, showing believers that they are not ordinary people but Kingdom citizens made for more. If we will grasp hold of faith and believe again, we can achieve all God has for us.

It is an honour to endorse this book, and I encourage you to read it with clarity and confidence, knowing your life will never be the same. Remember, you were MADE FOR MORE!

Prophet Dontrell J. Green Sr.
Founder, King of Glory International
Fresno, California, USA

Table of Contents

Foreword	1
Introduction	3
Chapter 1: More	9
Chapter 2: Made for More	19
Chapter 3: Made for More Purpose	27
Chapter 4: Made for More of Holy Spirit	35
Chapter 5: Made for More Fire	47
Chapter 6: Made for More Vision	59
Chapter 7: Made for More Wisdom	69
Chapter 8: Made for More Kingdom Wealth	79
Chapter 9: Made for More Miracles	89
Chapter 10: Made for More Faith	97
Chapter 11: More like Jesus	107
Conclusion	117

Foreword

It is both humbling and joyful to be asked to write a foreword for Bishop Greg Gill's book. When I introduced *Much More*, I knew it carried a message that would shift lives. Now, with *Made for More*, Bishop Gill has gone further, building on that foundation and calling us into a greater dimension of Kingdom living. If *Much More* impacted you, then *Made for More* is not just recommended, it is essential.

What strikes me most about Bishop Gill is his relentless pursuit of God's purposes. He does not write from theory, but from years of prayer, prophetic insight, and consistent service to the Body of Christ. His voice carries both authority and tenderness, sharpened by Holy Spirit and refined by a lifetime of ministry. This book reflects that same passion—awakening believers to rise out of apathy and step into the life of purpose, fire, wisdom, and abundance that God intends.

One verse that comes to mind is Ephesians 3:20, which says, "Now to Him who is able to do exceedingly abundantly above all that we ask or think, according to the power that works in us." This verse reminds us that God's plan for our lives is always bigger than what we can imagine. He doesn't just meet our needs; He goes far beyond them. Often, we limit ourselves by thinking too small or by settling for what feels safe. But God's Spirit within us is calling us to step into the "more" He has already prepared.

Made for More reminds us that spiritual comfort zones are dangerous and that God has designed us for transformation, adventure, and impact. In this book, Bishop Gill lays out a Spirit-filled roadmap that challenges mediocrity and calls us higher. Let this message stir hunger, break limitations, and ignite a fresh desire for intimacy with God.

Thank you, Bishop, for once again pouring your heart into a work that blesses and equips the Church. It is an honour to stand alongside your voice in this hour and to commend this book to every believer who is ready to discover that they are, indeed, made for more.

Joe Benjamin
Author, Publisher & Leader
United Kingdom, West Midlands

Introduction

Have you ever had that feeling, maybe after a spiritual high at a retreat, or just a string of good weeks at church, when you thought, "I'm finally where I need to be with God"?

Maybe life feels steady, your faith routine is set, the prayers come easily, and the questions don't tug quite as hard. There's a certain peace in that, an almost satisfying comfort. You're reading your Bible regularly. You show up for Sunday services. From the outside, everything looks… enough.

But then, something sneaks in. A quiet, stubborn kind of complacency. It doesn't announce itself with fanfare, but it settles deep, like fog rolling over a familiar landscape. Maybe you start skipping prayer here and there because work is hectic. Maybe worship songs stop giving you chills and sound like background static instead. Or maybe those big questions—the ones that used to send you hunting for answers, don't even surface anymore. Your beliefs are still intact, but your heart? It isn't leaping or aching for more. It's coasting on autopilot.

Let's be honest: it's tempting to stay right there, to believe we've arrived spiritually, that we've filled our "God

Introduction

quota" for this lifetime. We accept the idea that mature faith is mostly about resisting temptation and keeping afloat until heaven, less about ongoing transformation. Some part of us buys into the myth that once you've reached a certain level, you can just settle in and coast. After all, isn't stability what we're supposed to aim for?

But here's the problem: faith isn't neutral territory. When we stop moving forward, we're not standing still. Our souls, made for the wild adventure of knowing God, under the weight of stagnation. We long for more but convince ourselves that "more" isn't possible, or worse, isn't even necessary.

Have you ever caught yourself thinking, "This is it. I'm good. I know enough, love enough, give enough"? If so, let me pose a question that might change everything: What if believing you've 'arrived' is the greatest risk to your faith?

Here's something radical: there is no such thing as having "enough" of God. There is always farther to go, deeper to dive, higher to climb. The God who calls us is endlessly creative, constantly surprising, and desperately invested in shaping us into His image. He doesn't invite us onto a safe treadmill of "good enough." He beckons us into a living, breathing adventure, a lifelong journey of being transformed by Holy Spirit, day by day, encounter by encounter.

If your heart stirs at that thought, even a little, you are ready for what comes next. This book is not about giving you another checklist or adding items to your already busy schedule. Instead, it's about breaking free from the slow chokehold of spiritual routine and stepping into a rhythm that's vibrant, unpredictable, and drenched in God's presence. It's about trading lukewarm faith for the burning reality of relationship. And most importantly, it's about learning that God Himself desires, pursues, and empowers you for far more than you've yet imagined.

So, what would happen if you dared to say yes to this invitation? To shed the safety net of "just enough" and chase the "more" that God promises to anyone hungry for Him? Let's be clear: this isn't a solo expedition fueled by willpower. You are invited into partnership with Holy Spirit—the very presence of God who brings dead places back to life, who ignites dry hearts, who whispers hope when you're weary.

Maybe you've known moments of profound closeness

Introduction

with God, memories you revisit when things feel dry. Or perhaps you wonder if "more of God" is just a cliché reserved for ultra spiritual types, not ordinary people with ordinary struggles. The truth is, every believer is called into ongoing transformation, not improvement by human effort, but transformation by God's power. Holy Spirit is not a distant force or reward for the elite. He is the catalyst that makes spiritual growth real, rich, and lasting.

You may have heard spiritual life described as a journey before, but think about what that actually means. It's not a straight shot with checkpoints and trophies for hitting your marks. It's winding, unpredictable, sometimes messy. There are stretches where you sprint and seasons when you crawl. But through all of it, God walks alongside you, inviting you nearer, promising to meet you at each step with fresh grace, insight, and strength.

Right now, you stand on the threshold of something new. On the other side of your routine, your doubts, and your spiritual fatigue, God is offering the only antidote to complacency: Himself. Not as a doctrine, not as an idea, but as a present, transforming, joy-giving reality. Will you settle for yesterday's portion, or dare to ask for daily bread, daily presence, daily power?

This is your invitation. Refuse to let spiritual comfort lull you to sleep. Don't buy the lie that you've settled or that intimacy with God is reserved for the few. Decide today that you will not waste another season on autopilot. Open yourself wide, risk disappointment, risk discomfort, risk change, and trust that God rewards those who seek Him with all their heart.

Every chapter ahead is designed to help you reignite hunger, to guide you out of the rut and into the wild. Together, we'll identify the signs of plateau, explore what holds us back, learn to recognize the gentle nudges of Holy Spirit, and discover how to partner with God in ways that transform not just our Sundays, but our every day.

The abundant life Jesus offers isn't a myth or a metaphor, it's meant to be lived, tasted, and shared. If you're tired of maintenance-mode faith, if you crave more meaning, more joy, more God, then don't settle for less. Commit, right now, to join this journey. Bring your questions, your hopes, your fears, and your longing. The pages ahead are only the beginning. Ready to step through the door and find out just how much you are made for more.

Chapter 1
More

The Unbearable Smallness of 'Enough'

Have you ever woke up in the morning excited to spend time with God? Are your prayers heartfelt, is your Bible study fresh and alive? Over time, have things changed? Maybe, church felt like just another obligation on a busy schedule, and your quiet moments became hurried routines rather than deep conversations? Have you found yourself settling into a spiritual comfort zone, thinking you had learned enough and grown enough, that maybe this was as close as you would ever get?

It's easy to fall into this trap without even noticing. The hunger that once fueled pursuit begins to fade, replaced by a quiet sense of "enough." But what if that feeling isn't a sign of contentment but a subtle form of settling? Many believers experience this, where faith becomes more about going through the motions than seeking fresh encounters with God.

There's a subtle but powerful trap that catches even sincere, faithful adults: the comfort trap. At first, it looks like wisdom. You develop routines, find a church home, and settle into patterns of prayer or Bible reading. Routines become ruts, though, without realizing. Maybe you started out passionate, hungry for God's presence and eager for change, but after a while, the novelty fades. Church becomes an item on a checklist, not a fresh encounter. Morning devotionals blend with the day's noise, the words spoken but rarely sinking into a deeper place. You pray, but sometimes it's mechanical, a background noise before a meal or sleep, rather than an earnest conversation. In these quiet, ordinary ways, spiritual comfort slowly leads into complacency. It tells you, "You've done enough. You're right where you should be. There's no more to seek."

But believing you can ever have "enough" of God is an illusion that stunts your growth and dims your faith. Take the believer who once chased after God, attending every worship night, hungry to hear from Him, eyes and heart wide open. Time passes. Small disappointments creep in, life gets busy, and soon spiritual pursuit feels less urgent. The underlying belief settles in: seeking more isn't essential; it's for new believers or those in crisis. But by slipping into this mindset, you miss moments where God is offering new depths, surprising comfort, or needed conviction. You were made for more, and settling for "good enough" cuts you off from the unexpected freedom and joy that comes from pressing deeper.

Scripture cracks this comfort trap wide open. David's story jumps off the page with longing, a man after God's own heart, but never done yearning for Him. In Psalm 42:1, David writes, "As the deer pants for streams of water, so my soul pants for you, O God." These aren't the words of someone satisfied with spiritual leftovers; David's faith is marked by ongoing hunger. Despite kingly status and spiritual victories, he never stops chasing closeness with God. In the New Testament, Paul's life shouts the same message. He's a leader who never claims to have arrived. Philippians 3 shows Paul pressing on, leaving what's behind for the sake of knowing Christ more fully. Even with a lifetime of transformative ministry, Paul doesn't declare he has "enough", he reaches with every fiber for something more that only God can give. Both David and Paul disrupt the myth that maturity means settling, demonstrating that wanting more of God is the defining trait of grounded faith.

Spiritual apathy doesn't always look like open rebellion. Often, it shows up when worship no longer stirs the heart, serving others becomes a burden, or disappointment pushes you to withdraw instead of lean in. Picture a believer who goes through the motions for years, hardly noticing when devotion wanes or when bitterness slips in. The drift isn't dramatic at first. Over time, though, faith shrinks, there's less delight, less willingness to sacrifice, and an ache where there was once curiosity and awe. This mediocrity, left unchecked, eventually gives way to doubts or regrets, especially in hard seasons when only a fresh, living relationship with God will do.

The truth is, you'll never reach the "limit" of God. He's infinite, there are always deeper mysteries, new mercies, and greater love to discover. Trying to measure "enough" of God is like claiming you've explored every secret in the ocean after a single swim. Each step forward reveals another layer of wonder. A relationship with God is meant to expand endlessly, like discovering the uncharted rooms in a house you thought you knew inside out. You always find new surprises and a sense of adventure that keeps drawing you forward.

This is where Holy Spirit's role becomes essential. Holy Spirit doesn't just comfort when you feel shaken; He unsettles those parts of your life that have hardened or grown too content. Maybe you feel a gentle nudge toward forgiveness, a strange urge to apologize, or an unexpected prompting to step out and serve someone in need. At other times, Holy Spirit brings a quiet peace in the whirlwind, reassuring you of God's nearness. Holy Spirit is always inviting you forward, refusing to let complacency linger too long. It's both comfort and challenge, a presence that brings security even while calling you higher.

The difference Holy Spirit makes is concrete. Think of someone who, during a health crisis or deep disappointment, relies on strength and patience they can't explain. Or the person who forgives when every part of them wants to hold a grudge. That's not self-effort it's Holy Spirit's power, enlivening hearts and enabling real transformation (John 14:26; Romans 8:11).

A Call to Pursue More

A hunger for more of God should fuel each step. Scripture never treats seeking God as a side option for those with extra time or energy. The words of Jesus ring through generations: "Ask, and it will be given to you; seek, and you will find; knock, and it will be opened to you" (Matthew 7:7). He speaks with the certainty of a command, not a suggestion. There is no graduation, no final spiritual degree to be earned. Each moment offers the invitation to keep pressing in, to cultivate a life where seeking is woven into every day. When people draw closer, growth remains possible, and faith refuses to settle for yesterday's understanding or last year's encounter. This pursuit transforms belief from static agreement into living, breathing action.

Throughout the Bible, stories of ordinary people who refused to rest on spiritual milestones reveal the vibrant heart behind this call. Moses stands out, not simply as a leader, but as someone who wanted more. After witnessing miracles, the plagues in Egypt, and the Red Sea's parting, he still cried out, "Show me Your glory" (Exodus 33:18). He longed for deeper intimacy, despite having seen more than most could fathom. Elijah, weary on the mountain, voiced his despair and found the presence of God not in the earthquake or fire, but in a gentle whisper. These stories show relentless pursuit, a willingness to push past comfort to know God in new ways.

Barriers arise for all. Spiritual growth often collides with comfort, fear of disappointment, or a desire for control. Doubt whispers that nothing new awaits, or that change might cost too much. Some adults find themselves stuck, weighed by the routine of Christian life, believing they know enough. The world adds its pressures: endless demands, a culture obsessed with immediate results, and constant noise. Time becomes scarce, distractions abound, and restlessness seeps in. Recognizing these obstacles is crucial. Without awareness, spiritual hunger declines.

Identifying obstacles does not leave a person powerless. Instead, it signals the beginning of real growth. Writing a single thing you are thankful for plants a seed of expectation. Meditating on a weekly verse anchors the mind, renewing commitment in small, concrete ways.

The journey towards knowing you are made for more offers a joyful calling. Instead of treating spiritual pursuit as one more burden, it helps to see it as adventure, the kind that stretches and surprises. There is no finish line in the relationship; instead, there is ongoing discovery. God's invitation, "Draw near to Me, and I will draw near to you," stands as both promise and comfort. Each day, no matter how hard or difficult, becomes part of a larger story of being changed and renewed by Holy Spirit.

Choose to refocus again. The pursuit will hold new struggles, but also new joys. God does not expect perfection, but openness and persistence. Let the questions arise daily: Why do I want to be made for more? What is

God shaping in me now? Let these prayers, bold action, and trust that each step taken draws you deeper into a life that reflects His presence. By being made for more it is not a mark of inadequacy, it is the sign of a living, growing faith that refuses to settle for enough.

Now that we understand the danger of spiritual complacency and the endless depths of God's love, we can choose to live with fresh hunger and boldness. Instead of settling for routines or comfortable faith, let's lean into Holy Spirit's challenges and unstoppable power, embracing the adventure of growing closer to God every single day. There's always much more to discover, more to surrender, and more joy waiting in the journey. Take the next step, keep asking, seeking, knocking, and watch how your faith stretches and transforms in ways you never expected.

Chapter Summary

- Recognize the danger of spiritual complacency and refuse to settle for "enough" in your walk with God.

- Follow the examples of David and Paul, who never claimed to have arrived but continually pursued deeper intimacy with God. (Psalm 42:1; Philippians 3:13–14)

- Depend on Holy Spirit to stir hunger, break routines, and lead you into real transformation. (John 14:26; Romans 8:11)

- Embrace Jesus' call to "ask, seek, and knock," living each day with fresh expectation for more of God. (Matthew 7:7)

Chapter 2
Made for More

Breaking the Chains of Apathy

Some might think that those with real faith would feel fired up all the time, praying nonstop, motivated every day. What if that's not how it really works? What if feeling stuck, unnoticed, or unsure isn't a sign of failure but part of the journey? Somewhere along the way, many of us have bought the lie that our worth depends on how much we do or how big our impact looks. We forget that beneath all the noise, there's a deeper truth waiting to break through, a truth about who we are and why we matter far beyond what we can see or prove. This chapter invites you to rethink everything you've heard about your value and challenge the quiet doubts that hold you back. It's about waking up from spiritual apathy and stepping into a life that's made for so much more.

Uncovering Identity and Embracing Abundance in Christ

People sometimes wonder if their life really matters, noticing others' gifts or purpose and quietly concluding, "I'm nothing special." Maybe a voice inside says they're too flawed, too ordinary, or just not made for more. But from the first page of the Bible, a different story is told about every single human. Genesis 1:27 declares that God made each person in His image, not as an accident, but as a reflection of His creativity, dignity, and capacity for relationship. Just to be human is to be stamped with great value. That's the core of true identity, and it stands in contrast to what the world teaches about worth. The world weighs value by achievements or popularity; God measures it by His unchanging design and love.

It's easy to miss this when mistakes, past hurts, or comparisons cloud the mind. One person might think, "I failed once and everyone remembers it. How could I ever matter?" Another sees the public successes of others and feels invisible. Negative self-talk, ideas like "I don't have any gifts" or "God works through special people, not me," aren't just personal insecurities; they're beliefs that run straight against how God sees us. These lies keep dreams contained and generosity stunted and hinders us from realizing that were made for more.

Spotting these limiting beliefs is the first major step. Our negative experiences or emotions convinces us there's no point in trying. The harm goes deep: when we believe we have nothing to offer, we step out of relationships, hold our gifts inside, or dismiss opportunities to make a difference. Ephesians 2:10 says, "We are his workmanship, created in Christ Jesus for good works, which God prepared beforehand, that we should walk in them." That means every believer has potential, prepared and placed by God Himself. His standard is not perfection, but growth. The ongoing process of becoming who He made you to be is normal and expected, not reserved for spiritual heroes. You are made for more!

Living fully in Christ means standing in His fullness. Colossians 2:9-10 explains, "For in Him the whole fullness of deity dwells bodily, and you have been filled in Him." There is nothing missing. Being in Christ means you have access to His wisdom, strength, and everything needed to live with confidence. Imagine facing a tough conversation at work or a family crisis and, even in your nerves, sensing a sudden calm or the right words to say. That's fullness in action, not extra self-confidence, but Christ's resources working through you.

God invites every Christian into unique service through specific gifts. Romans 12:6-8 paints a picture: each believer has unique abilities, from encouragement to leadership to mercy, and all are equally important

Confronting and Overcoming Spiritual Apathy

Every believer has a core identity in Christ that overflows with hope, belonging, and purpose. But even with this truth, there are days when discouragement settles in like a heavy fog. Daily life delivers stress at work, letdowns from people, or the slow grind of routines that seem to lead nowhere. These common experiences can affect our passion for God, leaving faith feeling dry. Spiritual apathy often doesn't come as one dramatic event; it arrives little by little, one disappointment or distraction at a time.

The Seriousness and Cost of Spiritual Indifference

Apathy tries to come and rob us of our spiritual passion; it subtly redefines what is "normal." Habits change, but so does the heart. Engagement with scripture becomes occasional rather than essential. Worship shifts from encounter to obligation. Over time, faith shrinks to a set of moral guidelines or memories of former zeal. The tragedy is not simply missing out on excitement. The real loss is connection with Christ, the source of vibrant spiritual life. Paul challenged early believers to stay awake spiritually. He warned of teachers who confused the Thessalonian church, suggesting they had missed Christ's return, causing turmoil and fear.

Spiritual apathy can also surface in the desire to return to comfortable routines rather than follow God's new directions. Just as the Ephesian church had to face changes after the death of the last apostle and destruction of Jerusalem's temple, believers face transitions that test their dependence on God. When apathy takes root, it is easy to replace relationship with ritual, to look to past experiences rather than seek fresh encounters with God.

Daily Choices That Guard the Heart

Breaking free from apathy is not an accident, it requires intentional steps every day. Set aside protected time for scripture. Pray honestly, bringing hopes, disappointments, frustrations, and joys before God. Make worship a regular part of life outside church walls. Accountability with a faith-filled friend provides motivation to stay focused and realize you are made for more.

Consistency is the secret ingredient. Spiritual hunger returns as we pursue daily encounters in God's presence. These practical steps help the heart stay awake in response to Holy Spirit's leading. God calls believers higher, beyond apathy, into the fullness and adventure found only in Him.

Now that we recognize the truth of who we are in Christ and understand how easily spiritual apathy can creep in, we can choose to break free from limiting beliefs and daily distractions holding us back. By embracing the gifts and purposes God has prepared for us and taking intentional steps to stay connected with Him, we open the door to a life knowing we are made for more. It's not about being perfect or having it all figured out; it's about trusting God's plan for growth and letting His power work through our weaknesses. Let's step forward with confidence, ready to live alive in Christ, making a real difference in our own lives and the lives of those around us.

Chapter Summary

- Break free from apathy and reject the lie that your worth is based on what you do or achieve; you are made for more in Christ.

- Embrace your true identity as God's workmanship, created in His image and designed for good works. (Genesis 1:27; Ephesians 2:10)

- Live in the fullness of Christ, knowing that His strength and wisdom are already within you. (Colossians 2:9–10)

- Guard your heart daily through Scripture, prayer, worship, and accountability, choosing to stay awake and alive in God's presence.

Chapter 3
Made for More Purpose

Living Out Your Divine Assignment

Did you know that many people spend their whole lives searching for meaning and direction, yet still feel lost or unfulfilled? Studies show that many adults struggle with a sense of purpose, often chasing goals that leave them feeling empty or disconnected. What if the secret to lasting fulfillment isn't found in striving harder or doing more, but in discovering a purpose rooted in something greater than us? This chapter will open your eyes to a powerful way of living, one where daily choices align with a deeper calling that brings true clarity and peace to discover your purpose for being made for much more.

Foundations and Stories of Divine Purpose

From the start, the Bible teaches that purpose is neither random nor accidental. In Genesis 1:28, God blesses and gives us a clear mandate: "Be fruitful and multiply and fill the earth and subdue it..." This call is intentional, embedded in the very fabric of creation. It reveals that purpose is not something people invent for themselves, but a gift rooted in God's original plan for his people. When individuals recognize that God's purpose is part of their design, it opens the door to a life that is secured, meaningful, and full of resilience, qualities so many yearn for in today's world.

In our culture we are offered a different narrative about purpose. We are being constantly pushed to the idea that purpose must be pursued through personal success, status, or pleasure. While this sounds empowering, it often falls short. Many find themselves achieving goals but still feeling restless, and empty. Guilty of pursuing shifting standards of success yet unhappy and longing for a deeper significance or direction. The biblical worldview turns this thinking upside down. Instead of endless striving or comparison, discovering our purpose in God brings lasting fulfillment, a fulfillment that is not dependent on circumstances or the approval of others.

Embracing a God-given purpose equips people with clarity and peace, helping them to move forward with a sense of mission overcoming temporary setbacks. Instead of being lost without a map, people who accept God's purpose can face each day with confidence, trusting in Him in their choices, and value.

Consider how a divine assignment working like a compass, guiding our actions and attitudes. With purpose, open doors become opportunities to honor God, and decisions get processed through the lens of the calling. For someone who knows why they're here, even challenging circumstances can take on a sense of adventure and hope, they're no longer random hardships but training grounds for greater things.

Stories from the Bible help bring this concept to life. Moses, when first called by God at the burning bush, is filled with anxiety and doubt. He hesitates, overwhelmed by a sense of inadequacy ("Who am I that I should go to Pharaoh?"). God responds with assurance and provision, showing that true purpose doesn't depend on personal strength or credentials, but on God's empowerment and purpose. Moses' greatest impact comes not from self-confidence but from allowing God to fill the gaps. The same pattern appears in Esther's life. Risking her comfort and even her safety, Esther chooses to intervene for her people at a critical moment, declaring, "If I perish, I perish." Her courage is not reckless; it comes from a deep trust that her position is no accident, but a calling from God.

Paul who once committed to persecuting the early Church, is confronted by Jesus and given a new mission.

His story shows that no one is too far gone. A life pointed in the wrong direction can completely be turned around by embracing God purposes.

Understanding these biblical foundations is not just theory. At the heart of real transformation is moving from agreement with these principles to actively living them out. This process brings fresh energy, sharper focus, and endurance to weather life's storms. Once someone recognizes the power and freedom of purpose anchored in God's design, daily life naturally becomes more intentional. Setting kingdom-focused goals and reflecting on how each task fits within a larger story help turn this insight into ongoing action, guiding each step with confidence and hope.

Purpose-Driven Goals

Setting goals is not just for productivity, it's how you put your calling into motion. When you identify specific aims, they become clear markers of God's work in progress. Even when every detail is unclear, each small step counts. Goal setting, anchored in faith, replaces vague intentions with a steady commitment to God's unique plan.

Resilience in Purpose

Joseph's story offers guidance for staying steady in purpose, even in adversity. Sold by his brothers, imprisoned unfairly, Joseph could have abandoned his assignment or grown bitter. Instead, he persisted, committing to integrity in every place he served, forgiving those who wronged him, and choosing faithfulness when circumstances seemed hopeless.

In daily life, this means seeing professional setbacks or misunderstandings not as detours but invitations to trust and serve anyway. For instance, when a project fails, instead of blaming others or withdrawing, use the moment to uphold honesty and extend grace. This practice builds resilient reliance, the ability to keep relying on God and His purposes even when tested.

Jeremiah 29:11, "For I know the plans I have for you…" was spoken to people facing exile and uncertainty, offering the assurance that God's commitment remains even when the path forward is unclear. To anchor purpose in God's promise, meditate on God's word. Let your answers be honest, express doubts, hopes, or confusion. This is a space for authentic conversation with God.

Now that we've seen how God's purpose shapes every part of our lives, from the big moments to everyday choices, we can move forward with confidence, knowing that our days have real meaning and direction. Embracing this divine calling doesn't just bring clarity; it gives us the courage to face challenges, the focus to set goals that matter, and the peace that comes from trusting a plan bigger than ourselves. As you take each step, prioritizing what truly counts, setting faith-driven goals, and staying resilient like Joseph, you'll discover a fresh sense of hope and purpose unfolding in your own story. This journey isn't about perfection but about showing up each day ready to live out the unique mission God has for you, turning ordinary moments into something extraordinary, teaching yourself to walk in the much more that God has for your life.

Chapter Summary

- Discover that true fulfilment is not found in striving or success but in living out God's divine purpose.

- Understand that you were created with intention and called to fruitfulness from the very beginning. (Genesis 1:28)

- Follow the examples of Moses, Esther, and Paul, who embraced their God-given assignments despite fear, doubt, or past mistakes.

- Set faith-driven goals and walk in resilience like Joseph, trusting that God's plans will prevail even through trials. (Jeremiah 29:11)

Chapter 4
Made for More of Holy Spirit

Experience God's Presence Daily

Have you ever felt like something vital is missing in your daily life, a sense that there's more to faith than simply going through the motions? Maybe you've wondered what it really means to live connected to God every single day, not just in big moments but in the small, ordinary ones too. How do some people seem to carry peace, joy, and strength with them no matter the circumstances, while others feel tired, dry, or distant from God?

Let us explore a fresh way of living, a life marked by spiritual abundance rather than lack. It will guide you in understanding how embracing the presence of Holy Spirit can change the way you experience faith. You'll discover practical habits for opening your heart, ways to listen deeply, and the power of community support as you grow closer to God. In our journey, as we chase the experiences and learning to live steady and walk in the life-giving renewal that flows from Holy Spirit will cause you to know that you are made for more.

The Promise and Manifestations of Spiritual Overflow

Living from spiritual overflow is like discovering an endless spring running through the heart. When Jesus says, "Anyone who believes in me may come and drink! For the Scriptures declare, 'Rivers of living water will flow from his heart'" (John 7:38), He paints a picture of a life filled to the brim and spilling over with Holy Spirit's presence. Imagine the difference between desperately searching for a drop of water in a desert and standing beside a river that rushes by, always cool and always inviting. This is what Jesus offers, never-limited, always available spiritual refreshment that washes over all who trust Him.

Some people walk through life feeling drained and dry on the inside. A mindset of lack creeps in, it doubts that God will provide and hesitates to believe Holy Spirit really could move in our daily life. Instead of faith filled expectation, it brings a cautious attitude that suspects the well will run dry. This kind of mindset closes spiritual windows and locks the doors. The result is spiritual tiredness, with people feeling weak in faith, guarded against hope, and resigned to barely getting by. It's like living with limitations, bracing for shortages and saving every crumb of happiness for a rainy day. People in this place often feel like their prayers are bouncing off the ceiling and trying to engage in spiritual warfare without a compass. Spiritual lack shows itself when believers doubt when asking of God for breakthrough.

But God's message is totally different. He shows us that Holy Spirit is generous. An abundance mindset means expecting God's provision to overflow every to every need and never leave us empty. In the Bible, God's character is described as generous, giving grace upon grace and blessing upon blessing (John 1:16). This isn't just for super-spiritual people; it's the daily invitation to everyone who trusts Jesus. When a believer opens up to Holy Spirit, they discover the joy of giving, the boldness to serve, and the freedom to love beyond their ability. Instead of holding back, they release. Instead of being selfish, they share. Life becomes about both receiving and pouring out. Generosity, peace, joy, and strength start to flow, not only to them but through them to others.

What if you are weighed down by anxiety and a sense that you are not enough. Yet you attended church and studied your Bible, but the words felt flat, and prayer seemed pointless. In moments of weakness, you became critical and withdrawn. Then, during a time of prayer, you admitted your dryness and asked God to meet you in that place. Gradually, you sensed Holy Spirit's gentle encouragement, a peace you could not explain started flooding your mind. Within weeks, you find yourself eager to worship, hungry for Scripture, and even reaching out to a neighbor in need. Others begin to notice your newfound joy. What changed wasn't your effort, but your willingness to receive Holy Spirit's presence, opening the door to rivers of living water.

Maybe you once struggled with bitterness after a deep disappointment. You felt spiritually stuck and even stopped serving in your church. After a friend prayed for you and urged you to surrender your pain to God, you experienced a wave of release. Holy Spirit began reshaping his heart, you could forgive, hope, and risk again. You stopped seeing yourself as a victim and started overflowing with encouragement for others going through hard times. Your story is proof that spiritual overflow breathes new life, knowing you are made for more.

What unlocks this abundance for ordinary people? Practical habits can make a difference. Prayer invites Holy

Spirit in. Setting aside time for focused, honest conversation with God each day, opens the heart to receive. Worship lifts eyes from daily stress to God's beauty and power. Singing, listening to worship music, or simply thanking God aloud all clear space for Holy Spirit to move. These practices don't earn God's presence; they help us welcome Him. They train us to expect His voice, His comfort, and His direction.

Living from overflow is not about chasing experiences or emotional highs. It's about a steady, growing sensitivity to Holy Spirit's presence. As we cultivate an appetite for more of God, a deep longing for His nearness grows. This hunger draws us further into experiencing God daily, preparing our hearts for deeper habits and practical steps that nurture ongoing, life-giving connection with Holy Spirit.

Cultivating Intimacy and Growth with Holy Spirit

Abundance in Holy Spirit is encountered not just in moments that feel special but in the daily, deliberate moves we make toward God. If spiritual overflow once seemed tied only to dramatic worship or mountain-top experiences, its true power is unleashed when ordinary life is lived in constant invitation for Holy Spirit to fill and guide us. Transformation flows not from rare events, but from each Spirit-led choice, driven by daily practices, practical listening, and step-by-step faithfulness.

Listening for Holy Spirit is not about chasing startling signs or waiting for huge feelings. Real sensitivity grows in regular, undistracted quiet times. Create a space to prepare to engage his presence, where devices are off, household noise is low, and your heart is truly open. Start with a brief prayer, like, "Holy Spirit, I am listening. Show me what You wish to say." Let silence settle, resist the urge to fill it with your own words, and pay close attention as Holy Spirit begins to minister, leading us to a fresh revelation of how we are made for more.

Treat this listening as two-way communication. In prayer, speak boldly, then pause to notice his witness, like feelings of peace, or repeated thoughts about what really matters. For example, you might find yourself reminded to call a friend or slow down with a family member. Waiting for guidance often feels quieter than expected. Be patient if nothing seems obvious. Holy Spirit's whispers usually blend into your thoughts instead of flashing as lightning bolts. Over time, patient regular listening sharpens your sense of His sustaining presence.

Overflow happens when we actually move with what we sense, not just note it. Responding to Holy Spirit isn't about making huge, heroic decisions every day. Small, consistent obedience counts: learning to surrender, learning to be yield, learning to move as He leads. Each simple "yes" to Holy Spirit's prompting causes you to be more open to larger acts of faith. This forms a pattern of action that deepens and builds a reliance in God's active work in your life.

Waiting until you feel fully confident or until the "big" ask comes often leads to paralysis. Faith grows most in daily risks, apologizing after a mistake or offering practical help where it's needed, even if it goes unseen. Each time you step out, even imperfectly, you see Holy Spirit multiply small seeds of action into fruit over days, months, and years.

During a regular workday, you may feel a gentle conviction to share honest feedback with a teammate instead of taking the easy path of silence. Though hesitant, you choose to speak with care. Over time, he notices deeper respect growing in this relationship. Your openness draws constructive conversations at the office and leaves you feeling lighter, more aligned with Holy Spirit.

Overflowing with Holy Spirit rarely happens in isolation. God created His church for strength, clarity, and safety. Discussing spiritual experiences, life choices, or difficult emotions with a few wise, Spirit-filled believers changes everything. Clarity grows when you share what you feel God is saying and invite mature believers to help you listen and grow in those encounters.

Making important decisions, career, parenting, a shift in ministry, is not meant to be solo work. Bring not just your own ideas, but your questions to a trusted group, mentor, or spiritual friend whose priority is God's will above comfort. A conversation with others helps to know Spirit-led guidance from passing feelings or outside pressures. Community provides encouragement, gentle correction, and stands with you in the practical outworking of your faith.

Now that we understand how living from spiritual overflow invites Holy Spirit to fill and guide us daily, we can start embracing this abundant life with open hearts. Instead of settling for mindset of lack, we have the freedom to expect God's grace to flow generously through every moment. By practicing simple habits like quiet listening, saying yes to small nudges, and sharing our journey with others, we open the door wide for His presence to transform ordinary days into something truly alive and full. This isn't about chasing big experiences but about steady, everyday choices that build trust and deepen intimacy with God. As we move forward, let's step boldly into this overflowing life, ready to receive, ready to give, and ready to discover new depths of joy, peace, and strength in Holy Spirit's gentle wave knowing we are made for more.

Chapter Summary

- Recognize that life with God is meant to overflow with Holy Spirit, not run dry in routine or lack.

- Embrace Jesus' promise of rivers of living water that flow from within those who believe. (John 7:38)

- Develop daily habits of prayer, worship, and listening to Holy Spirit, creating space for His presence and guidance.

Share in community and obedience, allowing Holy Spirit's abundance to transform both your life and the lives of others.

Chapter 5
Made for More Fire

Living with More Passion and Power

Fire is one of the most powerful symbols found throughout the Bible. It's more than just heat or light, it signals God's presence, His power, and His ability to change lives. From the burning bush that called Moses to a bold mission, to the flames at Pentecost that sparked courage and joy, fire represents a force that awakens passion deep inside. It's both purifying and empowering, challenging us to grow through struggles while filling us with the anointing to live out our faith.

Let us dive into what fire means for your spiritual life today. It shows how understanding this symbol can help you cultivate lasting passion, keep your faith bright through everyday challenges. You will learn how to nurture and pass that enthusiasm on to others. You'll find practical steps to fanning your spiritual fire and see how living with this kind of passion can transform not only your heart but also your relationships and the world around you.

Understanding God's Fire and Cultivating Enduring Spiritual Passion

Fire in the Bible stands for far more than warmth or destruction. It is the unmistakable sign of God's nearness, a force that seizes attention and changes whoever comes close. When Moses encountered the burning bush in Exodus, the flames burned brightly but did not destroy the bush. Moses was drawn in by this strange sight, and as he stepped closer, God spoke, calling him to return to Egypt, freeing those enslaved. That fire was holy; Moses had to remove his sandals and watch, gripped by awe. The encounter was not just dramatic but transforming, it took a runaway shepherd and turned him into a bold leader armed with God's authority. The fire revealed a calling and gave clear direction that redefined the path of an entire people.

Later, at Mount Sinai, fire fell from heaven with smoke and thunder, wrapping the mountain itself. The people stood back, unable to approach, overwhelmed. This display wasn't to frighten for the sake of fear, but to emphasize that God's presence and holiness are not casual, not to be ignored or minimized. The sight meant business, stirring deep reverence and conviction. In the Book of Acts, flames appeared again, this time resting as tongues of fire above each believer. The room filled with wind, the presence was tangible, and ordinary followers received an unexplainable courage and empowerment. These flames signaled a new era, Holy Spirit breathing fresh life into everyday lives. Sometimes, that same fire arrives in life as a sense of intense clarity, a moment when God's presence seems closer, and old fears die away.

These stories point to moments today when people are caught off guard by God. A person may be sitting in silence, walking outdoors, or reading Scripture, and sense a new warmth, a call, or a sudden sense of readiness. It isn't always dramatic, but it's always real, an invitation to live with more openness and intensity.

The fire also purifies. Malachi's image of God as a refiner's fire speaks to cleansing, not just burning away for the sake of it, but heating gold so impurities rise and are swept aside. Spiritual growth looks like this: when life heats up with challenges, conflict at work, struggles at home, or internal battles, hidden motives or toxic habits come to the surface. This refining isn't comfortable. Start by recognizing that hardship may be part of God's work to shape you, not just random pain. When anger, pride, or bitterness show up, these are impurities exposed by the intense heat from the fire. The next move is a pure reflection, naming exactly what surfaced and how it affects relationships and faith. Finally, intentionally hand those "impurities" over to God, asking Him to renew your heart. For instance, when workplace friction reveals impatience or selfishness, the heat helps you own it and decide to respond with humility or ask forgiveness, clearing space for deeper love and renewed passion.

At Pentecost, the Apostles, empowered by Holy Spirit, turned from hesitant followers to bold messengers. Spiritual fire still looks like unexplained boldness, someone who never spoke about faith is now transformed by this outpouring and is moved to action with authority to call others to Christ and to share the message of the Cross. It's not just feeling inspired; the change shows in action, serving, witnessing, comforting, seeing the ordinary transformed.

A rekindled spiritual passion might look like this: a once-dull prayer life suddenly awakens. After months of going through the motions, someone decides to spend a time reflecting and reaching out to God. Week by week, peace replaces anxiety. You become more aware, more lighthearted with family, and start demonstrating the heart of Jesus because the fire has returned. Your daily life is now infused with new significance.

Sustaining this fire requires attention. Personal devotion is key. Begin with a nonnegotiable prayer time, make it a priority in your life. Carve out a Bible reading plan, focusing on just a few verses and what they mean for the day. How do they speak to you, note what is being stirred in your heart. Write down what you sensed regarding God's presence, and maybe even a struggle you may be facing. Make space for worship, even if it's humming a worship song during a commute or reading a Psalm while brewing coffee. These gentle, repeated actions help refocus your heart, keeping the flame alive when the initial excitement fades. The fire of God is always available, and Holy Spirit never desires to with-hold. Lean into Holy Spirit with complete surrender and open your heart for more and be ready to walk in this power.

To guard your flame, take inventory of your distractions. Maybe it's scrolling social media before breakfast, replying to emails late at night, or slipping into negative talk. Set a single boundary for each: "No phone before prayer," "Wait until after dinner for emails." Over time, these boundaries create room for spiritual refocus and intention, gradually helping you feel more centered and less scattered. These simple things can drain your fire; it can dim the anointing and steal your passion.

Daniel was known for his unwavering discipline. He prayed three times a day, regardless of risk or convenience. He was not moved by popular opinion or political regulations. He was bold, on-fire and pointed his face towards God. Maybe, like most, where you have let your passion slide, neglected prayer, avoided difficult commitment, or silenced your witness at work. Make a commitment, be bold, allow the fire to burn. Maybe it's time to be challenged to lead in your local church, invite your family to a Sunday service, pray before for friends or neighbours, or share an encouraging word with someone anxious. Actions forge the habit and fan the flames of the fire.

Passing the Flame

Having passion for God's work is rarely hidden. When you live and speak with passionate faith, that anointing has a way of showing up everywhere, at your dinner table, during a phone call from a discouraged friend, or even while waiting in a grocery store line. Just like Paul encouraged Timothy to "fan into flame the gift of God" (2 Timothy 1:6), spiritual enthusiasm can burst through the cracks of ordinary life. Paul didn't hide his fire; he poured encouragement into Timothy, challenged the Romans to "never be lacking in zeal, but keep your spiritual fervor, serving the Lord" (Romans 12:11), and expected this energy to shape communities and lives.

When you are truly available to God, passion doesn't stay between you and Him, it imparts into those you regularly touch. The Gospels overflow with moments where Jesus; even when tired or interrupted, stopped to help, heal, or stir faith in someone nearby. After being spiritually filled, the urge to reach out grows natural and almost automatic. That overflow happens best through authentic relationships, mentoring someone at work, comforting a neighbor through grief, or investing in the next generation at church.

Sometimes the spark is small, like a word of hope to someone who's overwhelmed. Small acts have large echoes. Picture the example of a woman who, after reigniting her own faith, changed the mood in her home by praying out loud before meals. Her family noticed a joy in her that they had missed. The result? A teenage son who started opening up about his fears, and a husband who started asking more questions about God at the end of the day. Her visible, simple acts created space for spiritual conversation and healing. Another story told of a teacher, struggling in a stressful school, who chose to send a daily encouraging note to a colleague. That single gesture caught on and other teachers started doing the same, slowly shifting their faculty's outlook. These everyday moments put skin and bones on the idea of "serving with zeal."

You may notice the change in others, but your own heart transforms too. A revitalized passion is contagious, especially when paired with action. Early believers in the book of Acts met in homes, shared meals, and prayed together; they built deep bonds by living out spiritual practices collectively, not just talking about them. Servant-hearted people, often leave impacts that travel farther than they ever expect.

Mentorship works in much the same way. When you intentionally pour encouragement into someone else's journey, you multiply your own faith. Imagine coaching a younger person, sharing your struggles, praying together, and celebrating little victories. Or think of the person who decided to reconcile with an old friend, risking discomfort in hopes of a healed friendship. Their step of faith rekindled trust, shifting the dynamic in a whole extended family. The willingness to go first, in kindness, apology, or generosity, ignites others to join in. Responding to God's call, no matter how small, opens a door for Holy Spirit to work through your availability. The fire changes the whole of a person. It transforms you and then you understand you are made for more.

Begin to look at your circle of influence differently. Relationships you might overlook, coworkers, neighbors, church members, even acquaintances, are places where spiritual passion is caught as much as taught. The examples you set, how you react to stress, how you celebrate answered prayer, how you apologize when wrong, feed those around you.

Now that we understand the powerful meaning of God's fire and how to keep our spiritual passion alive, we can take intentional steps to let that passion shape our daily lives and relationships. This isn't just about feeling inspired; it's about living with power and openness that others can see and feel. Whether through small acts of kindness, Godly conversations, or steady devotion, our renewed fire has the power to bring hope, healing, and transformation, not just inside us but in the people around us too. By choosing to pass this flame on, we join a long line of believers who've experienced how one spark of faith can light up whole communities. So, let's move forward ready to fan our own flames and share more fire with those we meet every day.

Chapter Summary

- Understand that God's fire represents His presence, power, and ability to purify and transform lives.

- Learn from Moses, the Apostles, and others who were ignited by holy fire to walk boldly in their calling. (Exodus 3:2; Acts 2:3–4)

- Allow God's refining fire to expose and remove impurities, renewing passion and strengthening faith. (Malachi 3:2–3)

Commit to sustaining spiritual passion through prayer, Scripture, worship, and bold obedience, passing the flame on to others. (2 Timothy 1:6)

Chapter 6
Made for More Vision

Seeing Beyond What Is

Have you ever felt like there's something bigger waiting for you, but it just stays out of reach? Maybe you wonder how some people seem to have a clear sense of purpose that guides their steps, even when the path looks uncertain or full of obstacles. What if the way we see things—our vision—could change everything about how we live and move forward? What if that vision isn't just about what's right in front of us, but something deeper, given to us from God? This chapter invites you to explore how seeing through God's eyes can change your perspective, replacing despair with hope when situations look impossible. Finding courage when doubts creep in, and the strength to take bold steps toward dreams that feel too big to chase alone. It's about learning to trust God what you can see. Moving forward and making the unseen visible allowing your vision to become your destiny and walking in the atmosphere of being made for more.

Cultivating Kingdom Vision

Abraham stood outside beneath a patch of stars he couldn't begin to count, hearing a promise from God that seemed impossible. He was already old, he had no children, and there was no one in sight. Abraham was called to believe that his offspring would outnumber the stars of the sky. He had nothing to work with, except his faith in his God. His hands were empty, but he chose to trust a vision so much bigger than his present circumstance (Genesis 15). This belief marked him as the father of faith, not because he had proof, but because he saw through the eyes of hope. Most people know what it's like to be waiting, maybe for a job breakthrough, healing, or reconciliation, feeling the weight of doubt when circumstances shout "never." Abraham's story reminds us that a God-sized vision generally means learning to have God-sized faith, learning to boldly hold onto the promise even before anything is seen. Faith, in these moments, lets us see what our eyes alone cannot. Faith is the substance of things hoped for, but the evidence of things not yet seen (Hebrews 11:1).

Nehemiah discovered the power and cost of vision while standing in the rubble of Jerusalem after it's destruction. He was asked by God to rebuild the city's battered walls. Can you believe, God would ask him. He had nothing but a connection, a connection with God. This is all that is needed. In the journey to rebuild Jerusalem he experienced all kinds of opposition. They tried to discredit him, many doubted, he had threats from the outside and often was tired. But Nehemiah didn't just have a simple dream, he had a vision! He prayed with simple faith and he and rallied people around this vision that God gave him. Even as opposition grew, so did the people's will and passion to fulfill the call to rebuild. When you feel pushback, and often do, while following God's vision, through fear, distractions, or discouragement, Nehemiah's story says: press on. A vision will grow your faith and determination. When you are at a stand still, when your world seems to be closing in, when your hopes seem dashed and un-reachable, God is reminding you that you are made for more. Rise up, hear God's fresh word to you and move in boldness towards fulfilling His promises in your life.

In every situation, Jesus lived with clear vision. His decisions, words, and relationships flowed from a single focus: doing what the Father sent Him to do. Through rejection, pain, and misunderstanding, He walked with clarity about His purpose. Instead of bending to public expectation or pressure, Jesus brought transformation wherever He went, through focused compassion and pure faith. This is the picture of Kingdom vision, centered, fearless, and unshaken by setbacks or crowds.

God invites people to live with sight like this, but it's not just about what's in front of our eyes. Spiritual vision starts with the mind's eye, or as Paul describes, with enlightened hearts (Ephesians 1:18). Seeing what God intends means moving beyond the surface, and drilling into the yet unseen. Just as Abraham trusted a promise and Nehemiah listened for God's direction, vision took root, and they believed the possibility of fulfillment without evidence. This takes more than a quick wish; it starts with asking God to bring clarity to our hopes, possibilities, and the path forward. Dream big. Write down your vision and make it clear.

Practices like prayer and fasting, highlighted in Acts 13:2, helps to produce this kind of sight. In early church gatherings, people were intentional to hear God's voice. We must do the same. God desires to birth fresh visions in our personal lives and that of his church. We need to set time aside, to be still, to have ears to hear and to allow Holy Spirit to make clear the path forward.

As we are made for more, we need fresh visons. We need new strategies to move forward to enlarge the

Kingdom and take back what the enemy has stolen. You have had your visions stolen. You have had dreams and visions for great things, maybe a business, a career or something besides what you are doing now. There is good news, you are made for more. Let yesterday be yesterday and today be a new day. Allow Holy Spirit to stir your spirit and let yourself surrender to his leading. Your obedience will produce fruit to the glory of God. Even today, you can experience new clarity by moving away from the distractions and pay attention to what God is already speaking.

We may have self-limiting beliefs, we may struggle with discouragement, and other "blind spots" that is blocking fresh vision in everyday life. Maybe someone keeps believing they're not enough to be used by God or worries that the setbacks and failures they've experienced disqualify them. It's time to face the giants, you were made for more. No weapon formed against you will prosper, let them fall. Real vision requires a choice to look wider, to look higher and broader, to expect spiritual possibilities in your life.

Seeds of a God-sized vision already exist and can change how you live. Taking time to move closer to God, release your faith and see clarity return.

Living Out the God-Sized Dream

Courage in living out a God-given vision looks a lot like standing at the edge of a river, not quite sure if it's safe to cross. Joshua felt fear when he led the Israelites to the border of the Promised Land. The land ahead was unknown, it was filled with giants, and he knew the responsibility for an entire nation rested on his choices. However, Joshua clung to God's promises and did not let his doubts determine his next move. He walked forward even before miracles happened and made real, the truth that we are moved by faith before every detail falls into place. The lesson is huge: God rarely gives all the answers up front. Following divine vision demands a first step, especially when nothing feels settled.

This isn't just old history. Maybe you are wrestling with whether to take a leadership role in your church's outreach. You may wonder if you are too young or inexperienced, doubting you have the right voice or skills for the task. Pray through your fears, you can trust in the Master's plan. God is faithful to fulfill His call in your life.

Perseverance is the backbone of vision. Abraham waited years for Isaac, trusting through disappointment and delays. Nehemiah faced endless criticism while rebuilding Jerusalem's walls, but he kept going without stopping to anger or panic. Their stories remind us that divine dreams often require waiting, enduring struggles or even pain. Maybe you have had your visions blocked or hindered, be encouraged, if God has spoken the vison to you, they will come to pass. Breakthrough comes at God's pace when we practice faithfulness, trusting that the journey, not the shortcut, reveals God's faithfulness.

Vision turns into reality by taking clear action. Think of some area where you sense God stretching your faith, a relationship, your work, your service in church or community. Picture what "success" could look like if God is involved. Write down one bold, faith-driven goal inspired by that vision. Maybe it's launching a small group for neighbors, forgiving someone who hurt you, or serving the homeless in your city. It could be starting a new ministry but make your goal specific and time limited. Real courage means action, not just belief, every ordinary choice, made in faith, creates an extraordinary legacy.

Now that we've seen how God gives vision through

faith, prayer, and action, it's time to step into that same kind of sight for ourselves. Embracing a God-sized dream means choosing hope when the future feels uncertain, pushing forward even when obstacles appear, and linking everyday choices to a bigger picture. You don't have to wait for perfect clarity or all the answers, just take one small step toward what God is calling you to do today. Keep your eyes on Him, trust that your journey matters, and watch how your bold faith produce fruit because of your vision.

Chapter Summary

- Realize that vision is more than seeing with natural eyes; it is perceiving God's promises and purposes by faith.

- Follow the examples of Abraham, Nehemiah, and Jesus, who walked in God-given vision despite opposition and uncertainty. (Genesis 15:5; Nehemiah 2:17–18)

- Ask God to enlighten the eyes of your heart so you can see beyond present challenges into His greater plan. (Ephesians 1:18)

- Take bold steps of faith, writing down and acting on God's vision, trusting that He is faithful to bring it to pass. (Habakkuk 2:2–3)

Chapter 7

Made for More Wisdom

Navigating Life with God's Insight

Imagine standing at a crossroads, confused by pieces of advice coming from every direction, all promising quick fixes and easy success. You want to do what's right, but it's hard to know which voice to trust. Sometimes, the noise is so loud it drowns out the small, quiet tug in your heart telling you there must be a better way. Life feels confusing, like you're trying to find your footing on shifting sand.

Many people face this struggle without realizing that there's a greater kind of wisdom available, one that doesn't go away with time or fall apart under pressure. There is a difference between worldly advice, and the wisdom God gives. As you read you will discover why turning to Scripture matters, and how biblical wisdom applies to everyday life. You will learn how to stand firm even when the culture around you tries to pull you off your path. It's about gaining clarity, courage, and peace by walking through life with insight far above what the world can provide.

Foundations and Application of Divine Wisdom

You are in a palace hallway and a young king named Solomon is standing before God and was offered the blank check of a lifetime. There he is, in his sandals, fresh in power, his nerves are on edge, and the future is set before him. Everything, gold, long life, victory over his enemies were all within reach, but instead he asked for wisdom. Wow! The kind of wisdom that cuts through the fog and tells right from wrong without praise or fear. Solomon knew leadership wasn't just about power or money; he knew real power needed clarity and humility; a wise heart bigger than victory in the battle. His choice wasn't just smart, it was bold. Rather than feeding his pride, he leaned into his need, admitting he didn't have all the answers. That moment changed everything for him and for a nation: Solomon's decisions brought not only riches and peace but respect, stability, and a legacy. This call for wisdom outlived him because he cared more about doing right by God and his people.

What's amazing about this is, that this isn't rare, like a one-time deal available only to old royalty. James 1:5 lays it out with radical clarity: "If any of you lacks wisdom, you should ask God, who gives generously to all without finding fault, and it will be given to you." There is no secret handshake, no hoops, no barrier to receive. Divine wisdom is offered to anyone ready to ask and is prepared to receive. The key is the asking. God doesn't limit the availability of wisdom. We often become the limiting factor. There is an open invitation. As a believer, our source of wisdom dose not come from the world. How can that wisdom solve a spiritual problem. It might sound appealing, but it tends to sound empty. It can leave us to have more questions than answers. You can chase after the foolishness of the world and still be wrong. But God's wisdom is pure, accurate and true.

Worldly wisdom often focuses on what makes you stand out, not what makes you stand up. Its nature is short-term gain, designed to cut corners, often empty at best. Think of leaders who ignored God's ways, like Saul, who let impatience destroy an entire kingdom. He lost his anointing because he chose not to receive the wisdom of God. He lost his life because he chose the foolishness of evil. Maybe you know someone, who chased after the world, they did not seek God and ended up in a life of despair and pain. Seek ye first the Kingdom of God, ask and it shall be given, knock and the door shall be opened.

Maybe you've been there, a fork in the road where everyone seems to have an opinion, but none of it calms your heart. Consider someone struggling with a job change, they are burdened by stress and by fears of missing out. They watch others leap for success and climb up corporate success to be only built on poor standards and worldly wisdom. They become stuck, anxious and exhausted, trying to think it out alone. But then, in a moment of clarity, they surrender. They find a quiet place, they pray, reading a Proverb about trusting God instead of their ungodly plan or their friend's "just do it" advice. The immediate solution doesn't drop from the ceiling, but a sense of direction stirs in their heart—a growing sense that peace comes not from the perfect answer but from walking with God. The anxiety slows down, confidence begins to rise, and finally, they act, not because all doubts vanish, but because their choice is connected in wisdom that runs deeper than the noise.

The Book of Proverbs provides a toolkit for life's every corner, packed with practical, no-nonsense wisdom. Maybe you are experiencing gossip at work. Proverbs 11:13 cautions about keeping confidences, helping you resist the urge to spread stories that don't belong to you. Or maybe you're tempted to lash out at someone who hurt you.

Proverbs 15:1 offers a solution, reminding you that "a gentle answer turns away wrath", wisdom that can change the air in a tense room. These nuggets go beyond simple inspiration. They become principles, like an internal compass that keeps you on the path. Navigating conflict gets real when you add biblical principles. Jesus urged forgiving others just as we're forgiven, and Paul's letters teaches simple steps for reconciliation.

Day-to-day stewardship means framing even your life and even your bank account with wisdom. Rather than cramming your planner full or spending on every impulse, take time to pray through your commitments. Plan for generosity, not just your bills. Set aside quiet time to reflect, rather than letting busy-ness rule. A wise life shows up in routines like small, intentional steps that honor God and bless others.

Persevering in Godly Wisdom

Daniel was just a teen when forced into a new life at the Babylonian king's palace. Surrounded by foreign customs and values, Daniel faced a menu of rich foods and wine he knew it violated his customs. The pressure was crushing. Everyone would be watching. This was no school cafeteria, but the heart of royal power. Going along with this would be easy, it would give him social standing, acceptance and even physical fulfillment. Instead, Daniel was willing to risk everything by refusing the king's food. He requested different meals and trusted the outcome to God. His bold faith could have cost him his future, but he held firm, and God honored him with influence and respect, even in a land that didn't share his faith.

Centuries later, Esther, another outsider thrust into power, faced her own crossroads. She could stay silent and blend in with palace life or reveal her true identity as one of God's people, risking her life to save others. The stakes were higher than being uncomfortable. Exposing her faith could have meant her life. Yet Esther used her access and voice with wisdom, courage, and prayer, standing up for what was right even when it brought fear and uncertainty. Her story is a reminder that Godly wisdom isn't just knowing what's right but acting bravely when risks are real.

Fast forward to our day, and these Bible stories can seem far away, but the theme of wisdom and courage for

God is urgent even today. We are being called to take a stand and are being called to stand in the gap. This cannot happen on our own ability, but it can through the wisdom of God in the face of a raging enemy.

Jesus said something powerful and reassuring about this. In plain words, he said when people treat you badly, or leave you out, maybe tell lies about you because you follow Him, you are blessed. Complete joy belongs to God's people. When we lose popularity, opportunities, or even or comfort for the sake what's right, they share in the same kind of reward God gives his courageous followers. Rejection and pushback aren't signs you're failing, quite the opposite. They're the evidence you belong to Him.

Not every challenge looks dramatic. Maybe you lose a client because you won't exaggerate your qualifications. Maybe a circle of friends starts excluding you because you won't laugh at cruel jokes. You might even face mild ridicule online for holding convictions on topics where most people disagree. Standing apart from the mainstream isn't about being stubborn or rude. It's about aligning yourself with Christ, who himself was misunderstood, rejected, and still chose humility over cheers. Refusing to join shady business deals or gossip trains isn't a holierthan-thou statement —it's quiet strength, proof you really live what you believe. This gives authentic weight to your witness.

Now that we've seen how choosing God's wisdom over the world's ideas shapes every part of life, from daily decisions to standing strong when the world pushes back. Now we can move forward with confidence. This isn't about perfection, but about learning to ask for God's wisdom as you face your own challenges. Remember Solomon's bold start, Daniel and Esther's courage, and the quiet faithfulness in your own life. You don't have to follow the crowd; instead, you can grow in putting God first and his leading through his infinite wisdom. The next step is yours—step out with boldness, knowing divine wisdom isn't just for Bible characters, but a powerful testament for real life today.

Chapter Summary

- Understand that true wisdom comes from God, not from the shifting standards of the world. (James 1:5)

- Learn from Solomon, Daniel, and Esther, who relied on God's wisdom to make bold, life-changing decisions.

- Apply biblical principles daily, using Proverbs and Scripture as a guide for relationships, work, and personal choices. (Proverbs 15:1; Proverbs 11:13)

- Stand firm in God's wisdom with courage, even when it costs you comfort, popularity, or acceptance. (Matthew 5:11–12)

Chapter 8
Made for More Kingdom Wealth

God's Blueprint for Abundance

We often find ourselves in a common struggle; what does it really mean to have money? Is it something to fear, to hold tightly, or to avoid altogether? Many of us wrestle with these questions, feeling trapped between wanting financial freedom and fearing the responsibilities or temptations that come with it. Allow me to invite you to consider a different way of looking at wealth. It's more than just as numbers in a bank account but as something deeper that touches our hearts, choices, and faith.

Biblical Foundations of Wealth and Prosperity Principles

Wealth itself is neither good nor evil. In the Bible, money is described as something that can be used for noble purposes or twisted in harmful ways. The true value of money comes from the choices we make. If money is directed towards selfishness, it can become a stumbling block. If managed with care, gratitude, and generosity, money becomes a tool for blessing others and fulfilling God's purposes. Lord make me a blessing. This difference starts in the heart, not in the bank account. Many people think that having money means automatic greed, pride, or guilt. Others view money with suspicion, as if struggling financially proves greater faithfulness. This is far from the truth. The Bible doesn't equate abundance with sin, nor does it praise poverty as the highest virtue. Instead, it calls believers to stewardship, taking care of resources as a trustee, not as the owner. This principle is captured in the words, "From everyone to whom much has been given, much will be required" (Luke 12:48), reminding us that resources come with responsibility, not entitlement.

People often fear money because of Jesus' warnings about greed. When Jesus says, "Watch out! Be on your guard against all kinds of greed; life does not consist in an abundance of possessions" (Luke 12:15), he's not condemning possessions but the love of riches that distracts from God. It's the desire to cling tightly to what we have or to anxiously chase after more that creates problems, not the possession itself. For example, someone may spend all their time worrying about how to increase their savings, obsessing over investments, or comparing their lifestyle to others. This preoccupation can cause spiritual emptiness, leaving little room for gratitude or faith. On the other hand, another person might feel embarrassed or guilty for having more than others, holding back from enjoying or sharing what they have, as a result they hide every blessing. Both mindsets miss the mark: wealth is meant to be managed wisely, held lightly, and used for good, not held onto out of fear or shame.

Looking at key figures in Scripture helps make these principles real. Abraham is a prime example. God blessed him with flocks, land, and influence, not because Abraham chased riches, but because he obeyed God's call and held everything with open hands. He chased God. His wealth became a sign of God's promise and provision. He was willing to give up even Isaac, his most precious gift, when asked. Abraham's story shows that trusting God with our stuff leads to blessing. Joseph is another model of stewardship. He handled Egypt's vast resources during famine, carefully organizing and distributing food for both Egyptians and other nations. Joseph's wisdom and character protected lives and revealed how Godly management, rooted in faithfulness, can turn hardship into hope. Solomon, known for his great wealth, achieved prosperity by first asking God for wisdom, not riches. His heart for understanding and right judgment brought him blessings that reached far beyond personal wealth, showing that seeking God's direction with wealth leads to greater blessing. These examples remind us that attitudes and actions matter more than account balances. God honors those who focus on wisdom, stewardship, and obedience over accumulation.

Misunderstandings about money keep people stuck in cycles of guilt, anxiety, and missed opportunities. Treating money as an idol brings disappointment. The love of money is the root of all evil. When we constantly want the latest possession, or feeling envious of someone else's lifestyle, can only create restlessness. Seeking wealth itself is vain and empty, becoming nothing more than a rush. Many with plenty find themselves lonely or dissatisfied. If God isn't the foundation of your wealth and prosperity, you are only building a legacy of wood, hay or straw. The Bible encourages contentment: "Keep your lives free from the love of money and be content with what you have" (Hebrews 13:5).

True satisfaction comes from adjusting our desires, not raising our possessions to match them. Gratitude and trust break the cycle of discontent.

Generosity transforms the believer's relationship with wealth. "A generous person will prosper; whoever refreshes others will be refreshed" (Proverbs 11:25). A simple act, like buying groceries for a struggling neighbor or giving a favorite jacket to someone in need, often brings lasting joy. The feeling that comes from seeing another person's relief or gratitude lingers far longer than a temporary thrill from spending on ourselves. It is not about the size of the gift; it is about the willingness to let go and trust God to provide more than enough. Real satisfaction is found not in accumulation but in sharing.

Financial Breakthroughs, Miracles, and Trusting God

Maybe you have sat at your kitchen table, staring at a growing mountain of bills and a nearly empty refrigerator.? Your work contract had ended sooner than expected, and the job market was weak. Relief seemed impossible. Yet, in that desperate month, strangers from your church showed up with grocery bags filled not just with food, but with special items for your children, exactly what they needed. Someone quietly covered your utility bill. The government deposits a check you didn't expect to arrive. Each gift landed out of the blue, impossible to predict or explain. Maybe you kept asking God for a new job, but instead, He gave us what we needed, step by step. God is faithful to meet the needs of his children. It's not his plan to see you begging for bread, you were made for more. Wealth isn't always measured in dollars, but often in its answers to prayer.

Holding tightly to money can feel safe in a world marked by layoffs, surprise expenses, and endless financial uncertainties. Yet biblical patterns show that the more tightly we grip our finances, the less room we make for God's provision to flow. Jesus' teaching destroys the instinct to be greedy, insisting that abundance enters a life when we stop chasing it first and instead prioritize kingdom living (Matthew 6:33). When believers release the control, it's wonder to see how their needs are met. They become participants in God's provision and prosperity.

Open-handed living looks like giving your tithe even when the numbers don't make sense. It's passing along a surprise rebate to a family in need instead of banking it for yourself. In some cases, it means giving away a coat or shoes you'd planned to sell, because someone else's need suddenly feels urgent. These choices trigger a cascade of blessing. The act of letting go not only shapes our character but also transforms our anxieties into an expectation of good. It's an invisible but powerful shift where financial pressure is replaced by faith and possibility.

Living this way removes the temptation to believe provision depends on my personal ability, skills, or control. God's economy is bigger, and more abundant than our best plans or projections (Philippians 4:19). The hands that give quickly also receive quickly, their posture reflecting the truth that God does not lack resources, and that His timing, though mysterious, is always designed for our good and growth (Romans 8:32; 2 Peter 1:3).

When doubts hit, remind yourself these acts of surrender are faith steps, not passive behaviour. Focus on God's character, God's wealth, God's plan and God's desire to bless and not remove. Use stories or testimonies and scriptures that ground your trust (Luke 12:24). As you continue, notice fear leaving and faith growing. Let this be the ongoing song, live with your hands open and your heart expecting.

Now that we understand God's true design for wealth as a tool to steward wisely and give generously rather than chase selfish gain, we can start living differently with our money. Letting go of fear and guilt opens the door to trust, where financial blessings flow not just from hard work but from faith and obedience. By practicing generosity in small, practical ways and choosing to see money as a means to bless others, we invite God's provision and experience peace even in uncertain times. This mindset shift isn't just about dollars; it's about transforming how we relate to resources, stress, and hope. So, let's take these lessons to heart, step out in faith, and watch how God turns our simple acts of trust in stories of breakthrough and abundance.

Chapter Summary

- Recognize that wealth is neither sinful nor ultimate; it is a tool entrusted by God for stewardship and blessing.

- Learn from Abraham, Joseph, and Solomon, who demonstrated that obedience and wisdom invite God's provision.

- Avoid the love of money, choosing instead contentment and generosity as the biblical pathway to true prosperity. (Hebrews 13:5; Proverbs 11:25)

Trust God's economy, giving freely and living open-handedly, confident that He will supply every need. (Philippians 4:19)

Chapter 9
Made for More Miracles

Experiencing Signs, Wonders, and Breakthroughs

Faith is the boldest step into the unknown. There's something powerful about believing in the unseen and trusting that miracles are not stories from the past but alive and available today. When faith meets action, it creates space for wonder to break through. Let's explore how miracles flow continuously from scripture into our everyday experience, fueled by trust and practical steps you can take. Together, we'll discover how to open your heart and life to signs, wonders, and breakthroughs waiting just beyond the boundaries of doubt.

Foundations of Faith and the Continuity of Miracles

The disciples must have been taken back by the words of Jesus, as announces his departure and then drops a promise that sounds almost unbelievable—"Whoever believes in me will do the works I have been doing, and they will do even greater things than these." This was not empty words. It was a bold invitation into a lifestyle of faith where the impossible, the God-sized miracles are expected. Some might object that only the early believers, those close to Jesus, could touch that kind of power. But a close look at John 14:12 shows that Jesus anchored this promise not in the Apostles' connection to Him, but in the ongoing gift of faith coupled with Holy Spirit's power. Every generation gets to live with that expectation. You can see this action of God's power and the manifestation of miracles in your life.

The Book of Acts reads like a rapid-fire highlight reel of supernatural breakthrough. Think of Peter and John in the shadow of the Jerusalem temple, crossing paths with a lame beggar who had known nothing but poverty and immobility. Peter didn't offer spare change. He declared healing, and bones that had never walked suddenly carried the man leaping with joy and shouting praise. Crowds saw, faith surged, and the movement of Jesus exploded through the streets and alleys. Elsewhere, simple items that touched Paul's skin such as aprons, carried healing to those who could not come close, while others saw deliverance that left onlookers speechless. Not only did these acts display God's compassion and power, but they also approved the message in a that was preached, pointing the sinner to God.

Miracles were never meant to be contained in the pages of history or to be stories of our grandparents. Today, stories are happening across the world of healings, many described by doctors as "inexplicable," or of violent households transformed overnight in answer to persistent prayer. In rural India, church planters have shared accounts of entire villages coming to faith after a child was suddenly healed of a deadly fever. In busy American cities, prayer chains have seen hospital rooms emptied of terminal patients who now walk out with new scans and fresh hope. These are not rumors, but stories with faces, names, and records. From all walks of life, people continue to encounter the God who delights in the impossibilities.

Witnessing or reading about miracles shifts something inside, doubt gives ground to possibility, and hope grows large. When we hear of the miracle working power of God, we are stirred, we are awakened with a new and fresh sense of faith. A faith that produces the miracles that we have been believing for. Your miracle will draw others to Jesus. Your miracle will inspire the weak to become strong, the outcast to return home and the forgotten to be found. Miracles is God's fresh word to a dying world.

Faith sits at the center of this world of the miraculous. The writer of Hebrews lines up a group of ordinary people, Noah, Abraham, and Moses each marked not by expertise or certainty, but by their determination to trust God and take a step into the unknown. The story of Peter walking on water captures this dynamic in action. Facing roaring wind and surging waves, Peter didn't wait for perfect confidence. He stepped out of the boat and locked his eyes on Jesus. He never saw the problem; he saw the problem solver. Though doubt rushed in and he began to sink, Jesus reached out and lifted him to safety. Peter's story is one of faith and belief in Jesus to preform miracles in our everyday life.

Many focus only on dramatic scenes and overlook the small, constant interruptions of grace that mark everyday life. An unexpected check in the mailbox when money runs out, a timely word from a friend that comes at just the right moment, a negative medical report that quietly shifts on its own, these, too, are works of God. Those small stories, when bundled together over time, create a personal collection of God's faithfulness that chases away skepticism.

As our hearts are stirred toward expectation, faith must join with bold steps and willing obedience. The miraculous becomes less an exception and more an atmosphere where breakthrough is normal and where we know we are made for more.

Cultivating Faith and Preparing for Breakthroughs

Attempting to walk in faith is the heart of seeing miracles break into ordinary life. Practicing repentance and humility opens the doorway to transformation and lasting breakthrough. Persistent prayer invites you to stand, expectant, on the edge of change, regardless of how long it takes. Inspired by the story in Luke 18:1, approach prayer with a determination that your faith is alive and will be heard.

Creating an environment of expectation starts with intentional choices that shape what you hear, say, and believe. Plug into a faith church, one that speaks of and teaches that miracles are for today. A church that allows the move of Holy Spirit in its gatherings and events. Becoming a part of such a place, will inspire you to release your hesitation, and allow you to receive God's promises. Remove cynicism or negativity, such as certain social media accounts or critical voices in your daily routine. Fill that space with worship and scripture reading. Engage in a worship gathering, this will stir up faith in tangible ways. Watch how these daily and weekly actions lift the atmosphere in your mind, heart and home, attracting the miraculous by keeping your spirit receptive and hope filled. Attract the miraculous power of God through your saturation of his presence.

Now that we understand how miracles have flowed from scripture into our lives today and how faith fuels these amazing breakthroughs, it's time to step forward with confidence. By embracing simple daily things like bold prayers, honest self-reflection, and surrounding ourselves with supportive communities. We than can make room for the impossible to become possible. Remember, every small act of faith is a spark that can ignite greater change—not just for us, but for those around us too. So, let's take that next step, trusting that when we combine courage with God's power, the extraordinary becomes an everyday part of our journey of being made for more.

Chapter Summary

- Believe that miracles are not only stories of the past but a present reality for those who trust in Jesus. (John 14:12)

- See how faith combined with action opens the door for signs, wonders, and breakthroughs.

- Learn from the early Church in Acts, where ordinary believers experienced extraordinary demonstrations of God's power.

- Position yourself with expectancy, prayer, and bold obedience, creating space for God to work miracles in your life.

Chapter 10
Made for More Faith

The Case for More

Maybe you had always thought faith was something quiet and easy, something you could tuck away for Sundays and special moments. But when life throughs one challenge after another your way, you find yourself feeling overwhelmed, worn out, and unsure if your beliefs could actually hold up. There are days where discouragement will creep in like a small shadow, when doubts will whisper louder than hope, and the temptation to just give up will feel so real. Sometimes it's not a sudden, dramatic attack; more often, it is the little things. The things like a harsh word, a setback, the endless noise of daily distractions pulling your focus away from what really matters.

You may wonder, how do people keep going when everything seems stacked against them? How do you hold on to something unseen and yet so vital when your spirit feels tired and your heart is full of questions? Your struggle isn't unique, many have found themselves facing invisible battles that chip away at confidence and peace, not with swords or storms, but through quiet moments of resistance, fear, and weariness. The kind of faith that simply sits on the shelf won't stand firm here; something deeper is needed. What does it look like to face these struggles without being broken by them? And can faith really be more than just a hope tucked away for easier days?

The Shield of Faith

Abundant faith isn't just about believing when life is easy. The spiritual life is a battleground, full of both promise and opposition. God calls every believer to a shielded and growing faith, not so it sits quietly on a shelf, but so it stands up to daily attacks and adversity. The Bible paints a real picture here, life as a follower of Jesus comes with fiery arrows, trials, and temptations. These spiritual attacks aren't dramatic or obvious most days; they slip in through everyday moments and struggles.

You feel the enemy's strategies in all kinds of ways, a sense of discouragement after disappointment, the tiredness that settles in when you feel like nothing is changing, or those inner whispers convincing you to give up. Sometimes, it's a sudden temptation to go back to old habits, or a busy schedule that removes God from your thoughts, distractions pulling you in every direction. The enemy tries to chip away at confidence using regular problems, hoping doubt and frustration will be louder than the promises of God.

Spiritual alertness becomes key. Passiveness lets fear and defeat come in easily. Paul's charge to believers is to be on guard, ready to always raise the Shield of Faith, not just during crisis. This is about choosing to pick up the shield, on purpose, day after day, even when you feel weak, unsure, or alone. Faith is not a quiet possession; it is a worn, tested defense that you keep lifting by choice.

Ephesians 6:16 says, "Above all, take up the shield of faith with which you can extinguish all the flaming arrows of the evil one." Paul is clear: this isn't an optional lesson. It's vital for victory. The shield he describes isn't just for blocking attacks; it puts them out. A Roman shield covered the whole body, and soldiers would soak it in water so the flaming arrows would be smothered, not only stopped. In the same way, when doubt, criticism, or fear comes at you, faith doesn't just dodge them, it puts out their power to burn. You might hear words from others that sting, or your own thoughts telling you that you'll never change. Raising the shield of faith means letting God's word answer those accusations. It's how anxiety about the future suddenly grows quiet as you trust God's promise to provide.

When discouragement hits, remember how the Psalms are filled with cries for help, and answers of hope. David wrote about walking "through the valley of the shadow of death," and yet refusing to be afraid because God was with him (Psalm 23:4). Jesus promises rest: "Come to me, all you who are weary and burdened, and I will give you rest" (Matthew 11:28). Maybe you've felt worn out, as if setbacks keep stacking up. Picture a runner, out of breath, tempted to quit. The promise is that God renews strength like eagles' wings (Isaiah 40:31). Sometimes, it means making a practical choice: pausing in the middle of trouble to whisper a prayer, declaring, even quietly, "God, I trust you are here, and you will see me through."

Temptation often comes when you feel least prepared. The seduction of comfort, shortcuts, or even bitterness grows louder. God's word is a sword you can pick up, but it's also the shield in your hand. "No temptation has overtaken you except what is common to mankind. And God is faithful; He will not let you be tempted beyond what you can bear..." (1 Corinthians 10:13). You can call out, "Jesus, you conquered this on the cross."

Walking by faith confronts every trouble, it gives solid ground and refuge. This faith isn't fragile or weak. Each time you trust, pray, or hold onto a promise, you build up a wall that can withstand real attacks. Even if trials continue, you rely on what Jesus did: His victory becomes your daily covering.

Living as people of faith turns your eyes from fear to hope. You can expect God to act, not just protect. God invites you to go beyond just defending yourself, to look for new things He wants to add, to expect prayers answered, and hearts changed. This shielded, abundant faith is active, moving forward, always hungry for more of Jesus and His living, unbreakable promises. Rise up, this is why you were made for more.

Abraham's Abundant Faith

Faith that wins battles begins with an awakened heart, sharp and watchful, ready for what comes rather than worn out from striving to follow routines or relying on sheer willpower. The world often links victory to how hard we try or how many steps we get right, but the biblical pattern challenges that thinking. Abraham shows a pure, unpolished faith, one shaped not by perfect behavior but by choosing faith when it mattered most. Believers can shift from constantly working to be "good enough," and instead find rest in the fact that favor and blessing don't flow from religious performance. Faith itself is the true channel of God's grace.

Peace and confidence start to take root where striving used to live. When someone believes that God's promises are trustworthy, worry about deserving love or working for answers begins to lose its grip. For instance, someone facing uncertainty at work—maybe an unexpected layoff or difficult boss, can default to anxiety and try to control every outcome, or pause and root their confidence in God's history of faithfulness. They might breathe, choose prayer over panic, and trust God's character instead of their own roadmap.

There's no story quite like Abraham's when it comes to faith under pressure. He received a promise from God, that he would have a child, become a father of many nations, at a moment when both he and Sarah's bodies seemed to guarantee disappointment. Year after year, nothing happened but aging. Friends may have offered advice or even pity, but Abraham held tight to what he had heard from God. Out loud, he would speak life over a situation that appeared dead. For anyone reading who faces pressing needs, a broken relationship, a financial mountain, a future that seems threatened, his example gives real hope.

Abraham's faith wasn't a secret feeling. He declared God's word, sometimes looking foolish from the outside, but he trained his focus on the promise, not on what he saw.

Faith always asks for action. Abraham kept walking, kept naming his faith out loud, kept preparing for the child even when there was no physical reason to do so yet. Acting on faith, not just feeling inspired, develops a faith that is solid and holds up under stress. Gratitude, obedience, and consistency are daily habits that turn fragile faith into something strong. Someone who needs financial breakthrough might keep giving a portion of income, trusting God's supply; another might thank God for healing every morning before seeing any change. These small, steady choices forge a faith that doesn't fade in delays or disappointment.

What happens when faith looks beyond the evidence? For Abraham, anchoring his life in what God promised unlocked far more than he could have brought about by effort alone. This is not a faith that whispers "maybe God can…" but a bold trust that expects goodness to appear.

When inner vision matches outer expectation, faith stirs up anticipation for solutions, provision, and even miracles, transforming both daily decisions and the long-term worldview of a believer. Trust becomes a steady lens and a driving force for hope in every area of life.

Faith protects us from life's daily battles and how Abraham's story shows faith in action, we can step forward with confidence, ready to face whatever comes our way. Building this kind of faith means choosing trust again and again, even when things look tough or uncertain. It's about holding tight to God's promises and taking small steps toward what He's calling us to, knowing that each act of obedience strengthens our defense and opens the door for His blessings. Raise your shield, speak God's truth over your challenge. Keep walking forward, because a faith like this doesn't just survive; it thrives and comes alive and transforms everything around you.

Chapter Summary

- Understand that abundant faith is the key to living a victorious and fruitful Christian life.

- Learn from biblical examples where trust in God released provision, healing, and breakthrough. (Hebrews 11:1)

- Strengthen your faith through prayer, the Word, and persistent belief in God's promises despite circumstances. (Romans 10:17)

- Walk boldly in faith, declaring and acting on God's Word, knowing that He is faithful to perform it. (Mark 11:22–24)

Chapter 11
More like Jesus

Becoming More Like Christ in a Broken World

What if becoming more like Christ isn't about trying harder or following a strict checklist? What if the real change happens quietly, beneath the surface, in ways you might not even notice at first? Have you ever wondered why some people seem to carry a calm kindness or an unshakeable hope, even when life feels messy and broken? Maybe it's not about perfection or big heroic moments, but something simpler: small choices, made daily, that grow into something lasting. As you read you will explore what it truly means to live as an image-bearer of Christ, transformation begins inside and spills out into the world around you, reshaping not only who you are but the way you love, forgive, and show up for others.

Transformed by Christ

Shaping the heart to look more like Christ does not happen overnight or through sheer determination. It's a real, everyday process of God working in ordinary lives, patiently and persistently, so that ordinary people are changed from the inside out (2 Corinthians 3:18; Romans 8:29). Sometimes growth feels slow, like the first green shoots in spring. Other times, it's as if something within finally gives way, and old stubborn patterns finally shift. The key is that Holy Spirit is always at work, even on days when we feel unchanged or even move backward. Being reshaped isn't just about following rules but about learning to rely on Holy Spirit's power, especially when frustration or failure creeps in.

When God's love fills a life, selfishness starts to let go, often through awkward, very human steps. It's possible, you once thought of yourself first in most situations, from how you spend money, to how you cut in line, or even interrupt during conversations. Gradually, you begin to seek Jesus' presence, and small changes begin to show up. In time, you find yourself listening patiently to a coworker's complaints rather than rushing back to your emails. That interaction hardly felt spiritual, but it showed how God rewrites habits at the most basic level, forming patience and self-sacrifice where impatience or pride once reigned. It wasn't passive; it was a new kind of strength, the kind built not on suppressing his desire but on forming new desires, ones shaped by love.

The process isn't about forcing yourself into a mold, but choosing to follow Christ's lead every day, even when it costs comfort. This looks different for everyone, but always means surrendering the old way of reacting with self-centeredness. It's possible you used to snap at your kids in the morning rush. After months of self-examination and daily prayers, you noticed your tone gradually softened. You still had rough mornings but noticed a growing pattern of humility, apologizing when you messed up and trying again. That's how real spiritual formation works: not perfection, but pure, persistent change motivated by Holy Spirit, grounded in scriptural truth and made visible in how we treat others.

One proven way to stay alert to what God is forming in you is simple self-examination. Paul called believers to "examine yourselves" not just to spot failure, but to see how Jesus is growing maturity in your life. This exercise is about naming where growth is happening and where you sense a deeper change is still needed. This isn't about self-condemnation but about letting God's truth shape you. Every small choice counts.

Christ-like love never stops at internal growth. Jesus made it vivid: "Love one another as I have loved you" (John 13:34). Loving as Jesus did isn't just about good feelings toward people you like. It's practical, meeting real needs, even at a personal cost. Sometimes, loving means forgiving those who hurt us. Jesus didn't tell his followers to love only those who were easy to love, but to bless and pray for enemies (Matthew 5:44).

Loving the "unlovable" shapes spiritual maturity in a way nothing else can. When Christ's love moves beyond thought into action, people notice. That's the start of hope shining out to others, and soon, you'll have a chance to discover how your life can become a visible sign of Christ's hope in the world.

A Life That Radiates Christ

The way believers live out their faith can shout louder than any words spoken on Sunday morning. When someone's attitude remains gentle after harsh criticism or when faith guides choices at work even without anyone watching, those moments can spark curiosity in the people around them. Imagine a coworker noticing a colleague carefully recording hours even when supervisors are away, resisting the urge to fudge numbers for personal gain.

Days turn into weeks of watching, and finally the question comes: "Why are you so honest when the rest of us cut corners?" In that quiet moment, daily integrity offers an invitation to something deeper.

In a similar way, consider the neighbor who always responds to rude remarks with calm kindness. Across fences and parking lots, sarcasm and skepticism meet patience, and the neighbor starts to wonder, "How is this possible?" Such consistent, Christ-like responses can slowly chip away at hardened hearts, opening unsuspected doors for honest questions about faith. These choices draw others in not because of polished arguments, but through authentic, steady goodness that fills gaps where cynicism usually grows.

People hunger for the real deal, longing for hope to be more than just nice words on a page. When faith shapes everyday reactions, it becomes a living testimony to the real work of God. Christ's presence shows up in Christ like business practices, choosing calm over anger, and being quick with encouragement rather than cheap sarcasm. These everyday choices aren't grand gestures, but they collectively paint a picture of a life transformed—one that invites others closer simply by being different in all the right ways.

There's a unique power in sharing a personal story of transformation. Telling a story of moving from resentment to forgiveness or from loneliness to belonging isn't just speaking facts; it's giving evidence that grace keeps changing real people, right now. Think of someone nervous to speak in a small group, but who chooses to share about forgiving an estranged parent. Others around the circle recognize their own pain in those words. The story's honesty opens up new conversations, as group members begin speaking about broken family relationships and the hope of healing. Genuine stories create a bridge between abstract faith and daily struggles, granting courage to those who feel stuck and doubt that change is possible. These conversations rarely happen through lectures. They begin when someone risks telling how Christ has changed anger to patience or fear to a sense of purpose.

Pursuing holiness every day means standing out, not by withdrawing but by showing up differently. It's seen in refusing to join the chorus of mean jokes at work, or spending an extra five minutes listening to someone vent when it's easier to scroll a phone. Sometimes, it means praying for a friend's broken relationship or for peace at the end of a long, frustrating shift. To be "set apart" doesn't require moving to a mountaintop or living behind church walls. It looks like someone who gently resists gossip and, instead, finds ways to encourage a colleague everyone else ignores. When others see selfless choices, they witness the quiet strength and joy that comes from living beyond just self-interest. This difference is not about being better than others or seeking attention, but about showing there is real depth and goodness because of Christ.

Living as a radiant image-bearer means making faith visible through daily actions. Small choices made repeatedly, can slowly turn heads and hearts. Goodness and integrity, when consistent allows the story of Christ's transforming love to move from theory to something others can see and, perhaps, seek for themselves.

Now that we've seen how becoming more like Christ shapes both our hearts and actions. It's clear this journey is about daily choices sparked by Holy Spirit, sometimes small and even slow, but sometimes bold and surprising. With each moment of patience, or forgiveness, we build a life that not only changes us but also quietly shines hope into a world that desperately needs it. This isn't about perfection or big ways; it's about showing up every day ready to let God's love work through us in real, practical ways. So, as you move forward, keep looking for those chances to grow inside and reach out with kindness outside, trusting that your steady faithfulness will open doors for new hope and transformation—this is why you were made for more.

Chapter Summary

- Recognize that the ultimate goal of the Christian life is to become more like Jesus in character and conduct. (Romans 8:29)

- Follow Christ's example of humility, obedience, love, and service as the model for daily living. (Philippians 2:5–8)

- Depend on Holy Spirit to shape you into Christ's likeness, producing the fruit of Holy Spirit in your life. (Galatians 5:22–23)

- Commit to an ongoing journey of transformation, allowing God to renew you day by day until Christ is fully formed in you. (2 Corinthians 3:18)

Conclusion

Throughout this book, we've traveled a winding but exhilarating path, a journey that began with gazing at the boundless nature of God and led us all the way to a transformed life marked by Christ's radiant presence. This isn't just about knowing some facts or having moments of inspiration; it's about weaving the divine into the fabric of everyday living.

Let's start where everything truly starts with God Himself. When you glimpse, even for a second, the infinite nature of the One who created galaxies with a word and numbers every hair on your head, it does something deep inside you. It wakes you up. As we explored how God's limitless power and endless love moves us out of any small, stagnant view of life. Suddenly, the ordinary isn't so ordinary anymore. When you let the reality of God's power settle in your heart, the walls around your spirit begin to crumble. The world grows bigger, more mysterious, and so much more hopeful. You begin to see that your life matters, not because of what you can do alone, but because God has chosen to work through you.

But recognizing God's greatness isn't enough if we're left powerless to respond. That's where Holy Spirit comes in. If knowing God's majesty is like hearing the sound of a magnificent symphony, then Holy Spirit is the conductor, bringing every instrument of your life into harmony. Holy Spirit's presence is more than comfort or counsel; it's the power source that breaks spiritual apathy and wakes up the sleeping parts of your soul. Some people spend years stuck in routines, believing that faith is just about following rules or keeping traditions. But when you allow Holy Spirit room to move, you can break free. Spiritual apathy melts away, replaced by a burning desire to live with purpose.

That awakening leads naturally to living intentionally and purposefully. Once apathy is broken, you don't drift through your days waiting for meaning to arrive, you chase after it, fueled by the awareness that each moment is charged with possibility. Purposeful living isn't about busyness for its own sake, but about moving through your

Conclusion

days with a clear sense of direction. Your actions become aligned with God's heart. Everyday choices—big and small— begin to reflect a growing understanding that your life's story is part of something much larger. The divine call isn't dormant anymore; it becomes personal, specific, urgent.

Spiritual fire ignites when purpose and Holy Spirit come together. This cannot be a passion that can be manufactured or faked. Spiritual fire is contagious, it spreads to other people, illuminates dark places, and supplies strength when you're weary. It's not just an emotional high; it's a steady blaze that persists through setbacks, doubts, and seasons of dryness. That fire purifies motives, burns away distractions, and moves you forward even when circumstances are tough. It's not about striving harder but about letting God's power shine through your surrendered, open life.

As that fire grows, your vision shifts. You start to see yourself, others, and the world differently. Divine vision is about seeing through God's eyes, not just perceiving what "is," but catching a glimpse of what could be. You become less focused on limitations and more connected to possibilities. Problems transform into opportunities for grace. You notice needs you hadn't seen before. Dreams that seemed too big suddenly look possible, not because of your own abilities, but because you trust in the One whose resources are limitless. Discouragement loses its grip when you remember whose vision you are carrying.

Of course, with new vision comes the challenge of decision-making. The path won't always be obvious. That's why godly wisdom matters so deeply. Anyone can make decisions based on logic, impulse, or popular opinion, but living in sync with Holy Spirit introduces a different kind of wisdom. You learn to pause, listen, pray, and discern. Wisdom gives you the courage to say yes and the humility to say no. It allows you to hold plans loosely, trusting that God sees what you can't. With godly wisdom, your decisions shape not only your own future, but ripple out— touching family, friends, coworkers, even strangers.

And as you follow wisdom, you will encounter yet another challenge: stewardship, God's plan for wealth and prosperity. Everything you have—time, talents, money, relationships, is a gift on loan from God. Growing spiritually means learning to manage those gifts well. Stewardship is never just about avoiding waste or guilt; it's about multiplying what's been entrusted to you so that

Conclusion

others are blessed. As you faithfully steward what you've been given, you discover deeper joy and contentment. Generosity stops being a burden and turns into a privilege.

Something incredible happens along the way: You find yourself open to the miraculous. Living close to God doesn't guarantee an easy life, but it does mean you'll witness things that can only be explained by His intervention. The miraculous may come as inner peace during chaos, healed relationships, unexpected provision, or sometimes outright supernatural events. These aren't fairy tales or wishful thinking, they're reminders that you serve a God who exceeds expectations and delights in surprising His children. When you embrace the miraculous, faith stops being a theory and becomes a daily adventure.

All these layers, knowing God's infinite nature, relying on Holy Spirit, breaking apathy, living purposefully, stoking spiritual fire, seeing with divine vision, choosing wisely, stewarding well, and expecting the miraculous, bringing us the best news of all: transformation. Not self improvement, not just becoming a "better" person, but true transformation into Christ's likeness. This is the ultimate goal and promise. The fragmented pieces of your spiritual life come together and reveal something beautiful: you become increasingly like Jesus. His compassion takes root in your heart. His patience colors your reactions. His courage strengthens your resolve. His joy infuses your days.

So where does all of this leave you? At the edge of a life that's both wonderfully ordinary and breathtakingly supernatural. You don't have to settle for a bland existence or a spiritual rut. Instead, you can step forward, one day at a time into a journey where God's presence is real, His guidance is sure, and His transformation is ongoing.

None of us arrive at this destination overnight. Spiritual growth is a process, full of twists, setbacks, surprises, and fresh revelations. But now, you are equipped with a biblical model, a map to keep returning to. Whenever you feel uncertain, reawaken wonder by remembering God's infinite greatness. Invite Holy Spirit to breathe life into dull moments. Choose purpose over passiveness. Stir the fire within by remembering what's truly at stake. Seek God's vision.

Let His wisdom direct you. Steward each opportunity with open hands. Stay alert for miracles, big and small. And

Conclusion

most importantly, rest in the assurance that God's aim is to form Christ in you.

This journey is worth every step. You're not alone, a heavenly companion walks with you, a community cheers you on, and a cloud of witnesses surrounds you. Keep going. Keep growing. The transformation set in motion by God's love and sustained by Holy Spirit is meant to spill out and touch the world around you. You are created for a life that shines with light of Christ Himself. Step boldly into that calling—and watch as you walk each day knowing you are Made for More.

For more information about
Bishop Greg D. Gill visit:
www.myeim.org

www.ingramcontent.com/pod-product-compliance
Lightning Source LLC
Chambersburg PA
CBHW020857160426
43192CB00007B/957